Pebble

Great African-Americans

Garrett
MORGAN

by Sarah L. Schuette

Content Consultant: Allen Ballard, Professor,
History and Africana Studies, University at Albany

Consulting Editor: Gail Saunders-Smith, PhD

CAPSTONE PRESS
a capstone imprint

Pebble Books are published by Capstone Press,
1710 Roe Crest Drive, North Mankato, Minnesota 56003
www.capstonepub.com

Library of Congress Cataloging-in-Publication Data
Schuette, Sarah L., 1976–
 Garrett Morgan / by Sarah L. Schuette.
  pages cm. — (Pebble Books. Great African-Americans)
 Includes bibliographical references and index.
 Summary: "Simple text and photographs present the life of Garrett Morgan, an African-American
inventor and entrepreneur"— Provided by publisher.
 ISBN 978-1-4914-0504-8 (library binding) — ISBN 978-1-4914-0510-9 (pbk.) — ISBN 978-1-
4914-0516-1 (ebook pdf)
1. Morgan, Garrett A., 1877–1963—Juvenile literature. 2. African American inventors—
Biography—Juvenile literature. 3. African American businesspeople—Biography—Juvenile
literature. I. Title.
 TJ140.M67S38 2015
 609.2–dc23
 [B]   2014007344

Editorial Credits
Nikki Bruno Clapper, editor; Terri Poburka, designer; Kelly Garvin, media researcher;
Laura Manthe, production specialist

Photo Credits
Special Collections, Cleveland State University Library: 10, 12, 18; Getty Images, Inc./Archive
Photos, cover, 20; Library of Congress: 8; Shutterstock/Marfo, cover art; SuperStock/Universal
Image Group, 6; Wikimedia: 4, 14, US Patent and Trademark Office, 16

Note to Parents and Teachers

The Great African-Americans set supports national curriculum standards for
social studies related to people, places, and environments. This book describes and
illustrates Garrett Morgan. The images support early readers in understanding
the text. The repetition of words and phrases helps early readers learn new words.
This book also introduces early readers to subject-specific vocabulary words, which
are defined in the Glossary section. Early readers may need assistance to read
some words and to use the Table of Contents, Glossary, Read More, Internet Sites,
Critical Thinking Using the Common Core, and Index sections of the book.

Printed in the United States of America in Stevens Point, Wisconsin.
032014   008092WZF14

Table of Contents

1877

born

Early Years

Garrett Morgan was a famous inventor. He was born in Kentucky in 1877. Garrett had 10 brothers and sisters. His parents were freed slaves.

a street in Cleveland, 1901

1877

born

Garrett left school after sixth grade. At age 14 he moved to Ohio in search of a job. Garrett settled in the city of Cleveland. He worked at a sewing machine company.

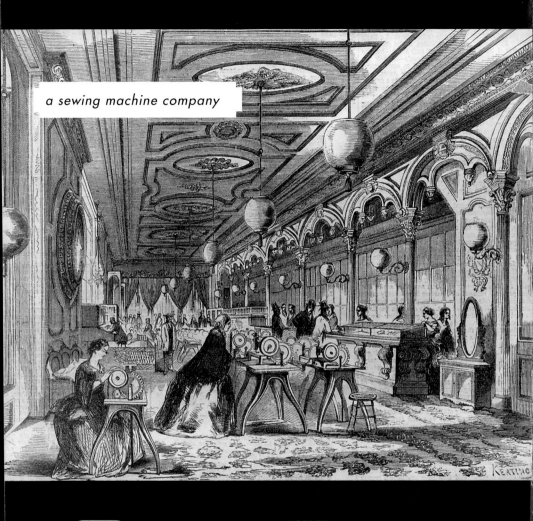

a sewing machine company

1877
born

1907
opens repair
shop

Grown-Up Garrett

Garrett studied machines
all day at work. He invented
a new sewing machine
and a belt fastener. In 1907
he opened a repair shop
for sewing equipment.

1877
born

1907
opens repair shop

1908
marries Mary Anne Hassek

In 1908 Garrett married
Mary Anne Hassek.
Garrett and Mary Anne
opened a tailor shop.
Garrett also sold a cream
that straightened hair.
He became wealthy.

Garrett wearing
his safety hood

1877

born

1907

opens repair
shop

1908

marries Mary
Anne Hassek

Middle Years

Garrett's most famous invention was a safety hood. It helped firefighters breathe safely in smoky air. Garrett's safety hood saved many lives. Soldiers used it during World War I.

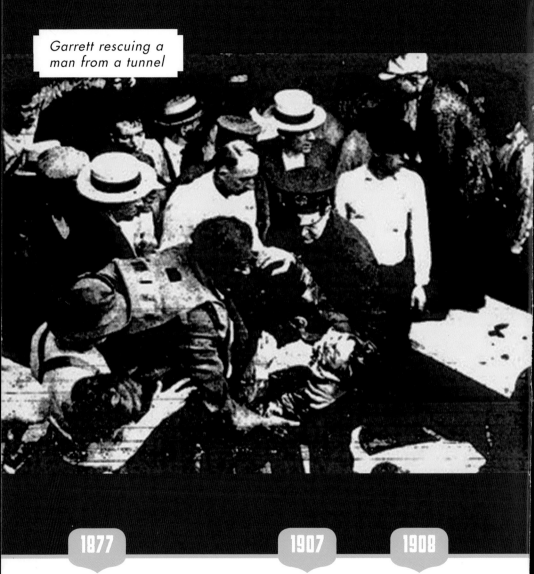

Garrett rescuing a man from a tunnel

1877

born

1907

opens repair shop

1908

marries Mary Anne Hassek

In 1916 there was an explosion in a tunnel under Lake Erie. Garrett and his brother rushed to the tunnel. They put on safety hoods, went into the tunnel, and saved two men's lives.

1916
saves men
in tunnel

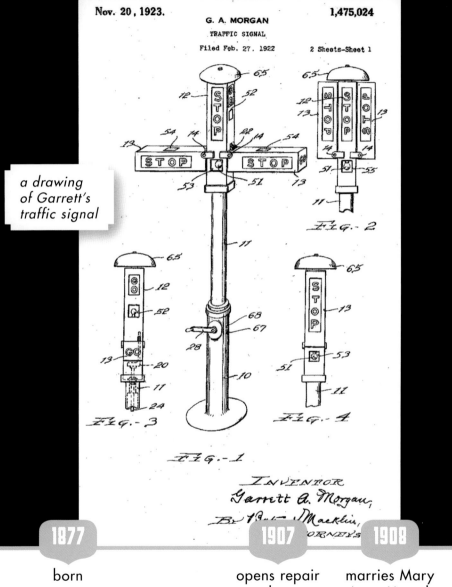

a drawing of Garrett's traffic signal

In the 1920s there were a lot of car accidents. Garrett wanted the streets to be safer. In 1923 he invented a traffic signal. His signals later became the traffic lights we use today.

1916
saves men
in tunnel

1923
invents traffic
signal

1877
born

1907
opens repair
shop

1908
marries Mary
Anne Hassek

Later Years

Garrett was a leader in the

African-American community.

He started a newspaper

called the *Cleveland Call.*

He also gave money to

African-American colleges.

1916
saves men
in tunnel

1923
invents traffic
signal

1877

born

1907

opens repair
shop

1908

marries Mary
Anne Hassek

After a lifetime of inventing, Garrett died in 1963. He is best known for his safety hood and traffic signal. These inventions made the world a safer place.

1916
saves men
in tunnel

1923
invents traffic
signal

1963
dies

Glossary

community—a group of people who live in the same area

explosion—a moment when something blows apart with a loud bang and great force

fastener—something that attaches two things to each other

invent—to think up and make something new

inventor—a person who thinks up and makes something new

settle—to make a place your home

slave—a person who is owned by another person

tailor—a person who sews clothing

World War I (1914–1918)—the war between the Central Powers (Germany, Austria-Hungary, and Turkey) and the Allied Powers (mainly France, Great Britain, Russia, Italy, Japan, and the United States)

Read More

Abdul-Jabbar, Kareem. *What Color Is My World?: The Lost History of African-American Inventors.* Somerville, Mass.: Candlewick, 2012.

Greenfield, Eloise. *The Great Migration: Journey to the North.* New York: Amistad, 2011.

Ready, Dee. *Firefighters Help.* Pebble Books: Our Community Helpers. North Mankato, Minn.: Capstone Press, 2013.

Internet Sites

FactHound offers a safe, fun way to find Internet sites related to this book. All of the sites on FactHound have been researched by our staff.

Here's all you do:
Visit *www.facthound.com*
Type in this code: 9781491405048

Check out projects, games and lots more at
www.capstonekids.com

Critical Thinking Using the Common Core

1. What kinds of businesses did Garrett Morgan start? (Key Ideas and Details)

2. What kinds of information about Garrett Morgan can you find in the chapter called "Early Years"? (Craft and Structure)

Index

Word Count: 257
Grade: 1
Early-Intervention Level: 22